CAMBRIDGE ENGLISH
Worldwide

Listening and Speaking Pack One

ANDREW LITTLEJOHN & DIANA HICKS

CAMBRIDGE
UNIVERSITY PRESS

PUBLISHED BY THE PRESS SYNDICATE OF THE UNIVERSITY OF CAMBRIDGE
The Pitt Building, Trumpington Street, Cambridge CB2 1RP

CAMBRIDGE UNIVERSITY PRESS
The Edinburgh Building, Cambridge CB2 2RU, United Kingdom
40 West 20th Street, New York, NY 10011-4211, USA
10 Stamford Road, Oakleigh, Melbourne 3166, Australia

First Published 1999

Printed in United Kingdom at the University Press, Cambridge.

ISBN 0 521 64508 5 Listening and Speaking Pack
ISBN 0 521 64512 3 Student's Book
ISBN 0 521 64511 5 Workbook
ISBN 0 521 64510 7 Teacher's Book
ISBN 0 521 64509 3 Class Cassette Set

Contents

1 Welcome to English!

Introductions;
pronunciation: /iːn/ and /ɪ/;
numbers; vocabulary; song

1   Talk to David

Introductions: writing and speaking

Write your answers to David's questions.

DAVID: Hi, my name's David. What's your name?

YOU: ....

DAVID: Oh. How do you spell that?

YOU: ....

DAVID: That's a nice name. How old are you? I'm 12.

YOU: ....

DAVID: Which school do you go to?

YOU: ....

DAVID.   Do you? I go to Central Secondary School. Where do you live?

YOU: ....

DAVID: Really? I live in Ireland. What language do you speak?

YOU: ....

DAVID: Your English is very good!

▭ Now talk to David on the cassette.

2   '-een' and '-y'

Pronunciation: /iːn/ and /ɪ/

Don't forget the 'n' with these numbers:

13 thir**teen**   14 four**teen**   15 fif**teen**   16 six**teen**

17 seven**teen**   18 eigh**teen**   19 nine**teen**

These numbers haven't got an 'n':

30 thirty   40 forty   50 fifty   60 sixty   70 seventy

80 eighty   90 ninety

▭ Listen to the cassette and say the numbers.

13	30	16	60	18	80
14	40	17	70	19	90
15	50				

3 A maths puzzle

🔲 Listen. Tick (√) the number you hear.

13 ☐ 30 ☐	18 ☐ 80 ☐	15 ☐ 50 ☐
14 ☐ 40 ☐	17 ☐ 70 ☐	19 ☐ 90 ☐
16 ☐ 60 ☐		

Now add (+) the numbers with a tick, and divide the total by two (/2).

What's your answer? ....

Your teacher has the correct answer.

4 Talk to Linda

Meeting people

Write your answers to Linda's questions.

LINDA: Hello.

YOU: ....

LINDA: My name's Linda Collier. What's your name?

YOU: ....

LINDA: I'm English. Are you English?

YOU: ....

LINDA: I'm thirteen years old. How old are you?

YOU: ....

LINDA: I live in Manchester. Where do you live?

YOU: ....

🔲 Now talk to Linda on the cassette.

5 Sing a song! I'm so happy

🔲 See page 90 in your Student's Book
for the words to 'I'm so happy'.

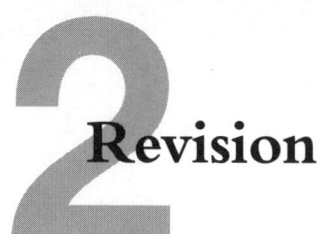

2 Revision

---

1 On the telephone

 Talk to Ahmed on the telephone in Pakistan.

Adjectives; 'have/has got'

AHMED: Hi. How are you?

YOU: ....

AHMED: What do you look like? I've got brown eyes. What colour are your eyes?

YOU: ....

AHMED: Have you got long hair?

YOU: ....

AHMED: I've got straight hair. Have you got curly hair or straight hair?

YOU: ....

AHMED: Can you send me a picture?

YOU: ....

AHMED: I've got a lot of homework tonight. Talk to you soon. Bye!

YOU: ....

---

2 At the airport

Talk to the man at San Francisco airport.

Personal details; social language

MAN: Welcome to San Francisco.

YOU: ....

MAN: Can you tell me your name please?

YOU: ....

MAN: And your telephone number?

YOU: ....

MAN: OK. Thanks. Your address?

YOU: ....

MAN: And your first language is ...?

YOU: ....

MAN: How old are you?

YOU: ....

MAN: Thanks. Bye.

YOU: ....

3 Topic Around our school

---

1 Say it clearly!

/æm/ *(am)*
/aɪm/ *(I'm)*

There are two ways to say 'I am' in English. Listen. Say these sentences.

Yes, I am.   No, I'm not.

Answer David's questions.

DAVID: Hi, are you on holiday today?

YOU: ....

DAVID: Oh! I'm on holiday today. I'm on holiday for eight weeks in the summer. Are you on holiday in July and August?

YOU: ....

DAVID: Really? I'm on holiday in February too. Are you at school then?

YOU: ....

DAVID: Your English is very good. Are you learning English at school?

YOU: ....

DAVID: Excellent! Talk to you soon. Bye!

---

2 In the bags

Days, subjects

Listen to a letter from Maria. Write the days next to the bags.

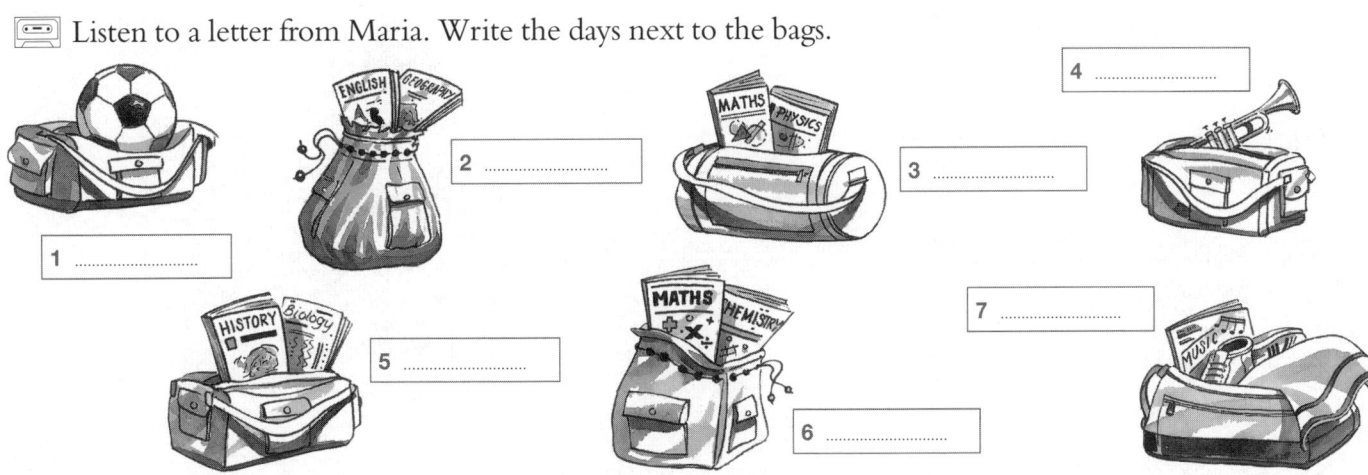

---

3 Sing a song! In my town, in the countryside

See page 90 in your Student's Book for the words to 'In my town, in the countryside'.

Extension

For more work on Unit 3, see Extension Exercise 1 on page 20.

Language focus

1 Say it clearly!

There are many words with 'th' in English.
Can you write four here?

....

....

Can you say them?
▭ Listen. Say the sentences.

Put your tongue between your teeth!

> This is the Brown family.
> They have three children.
> This is _____ the father.
> This is the mother.
> This is Elizabeth.
> This is Matthew.
> This is Arthur.

/ð/ (*th*is)
/θ/ (*th*ink)

2 In the shop

Going shopping

▭ Talk to the shop assistant. Look at the pictures and buy two things.

> Excuse me, how much are these jeans?
>
> How much is this bag?
>
> That's expensive!
>
> How much are these jeans?
>
> Can I pay for the jeans and the bag please?
>
> Here you are.

YOU: .... ?

SHOP ASSISTANT: £250.

YOU: .... !!!

SHOP ASSISTANT: They're very good.

YOU: .... ?

SHOP ASSISTANT: They're £15.

YOU: .... ?

SHOP ASSISTANT: That's £4.50.

YOU: ....

SHOP ASSISTANT: That's £15 and £4.50. That's £19.50 please.

YOU: ....

SHOP ASSISTANT: Thank you.

Extension

For more work on Unit 4, see Extension Exercise 2 on page 21.

Topic **In the wild**

---

1 Say it clearly!

/s/, /z/ and /ɪz/

🔊 There are three ways to say '–s' in English. Listen and say the words.

's' sound: cats bats sharks parrots
'z' sound: cows lions dolphins whales tigers penguins bees
'iz' sound: horses ostriches rhinoceroses

🔊 Put these words in the correct column. Check your answers with the cassette.

maps boxes books leaves
glasses shops rivers farms
hours towns buses

's' sound	'z' sound	'iz' sound

---

2 Talk to David

Animals

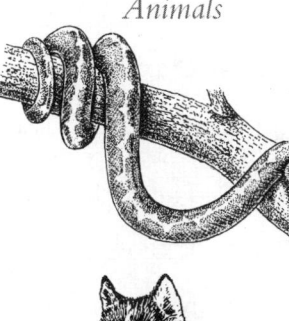

🔊 Write your answers to David's questions. Then talk to him on the cassette.

DAVID: Hello. My name's David. What's your name?

YOU: ....

DAVID: Have you got any pets at home?

YOU: ....

DAVID: I've got a snake! A long, black snake. It's a python. Do you like snakes?

YOU: ....

DAVID: Well, I think snakes are beautiful. I've also got a cat. His name's Izzy.
He sleeps all day. Do you like cats?

YOU: ....

DAVID: What about horses? I can ride a horse. Can you?

YOU: ....

DAVID: What's your favourite animal?

YOU: ....

DAVID: That's my favourite animal, too!

---

3 Sing a song! **Wimoweh**

🔊 See page 90 in the Student's Book for the words to 'Wimoweh'.

6 Language focus

---

1 Say it clearly!   /s/, /z/ *and* /ɪz/

Remember the three ways to say 's' in English: /s/ as in 'it's', /z/ as in 'is' and /ɪz/ as in 'boxes'.

Listen. Write /s/, /z/ or /ɪz/.

Now you say it. Listen to the cassette again.

2 Talk to David   *Inviting*

Look at the pictures and talk to David.

DAVID:	Hello. What's your name?
YOU:	....
DAVID:	My name's David.
YOU:	.... ?
DAVID:	No, thanks. I don't like chocolate.
YOU:	.... ?
DAVID:	I live in Hill Road.
YOU:	.... *after school* ?
DAVID:	I don't know. I can ask my mum.
YOU:	.... ?
DAVID:	It's 675432.
YOU:	I can ring you later.
DAVID:	Great!

Extension

For more work on Unit 6, see Extension Exercises 3 and 4 on pages 21–22.

7 Topic Food matters

1 Talk to Linda

Meals

Write your answers to Linda's questions. Tell her about your lunch or dinner.

LINDA: Hello, how are you?

YOU: ....

LINDA: I'm fine. It's nearly time for lunch. Do you know what I have for lunch?

YOU: ....

LINDA: I have vegetable soup and fresh bread. It's delicious! What do you have?

YOU: ....

LINDA: Mmmmm, I like that too. How many meals do you eat every day?

YOU: ....

LINDA: I usually have three meals a day. Do you eat between meals?

YOU: ....

LINDA: Sometimes I have an apple or a biscuit. Oh, look at the time! It's time to eat! Bye!

YOU: ....

▭ Talk to Linda on the cassette.

2 Say it clearly!

/iː/

▭ 'Cheese' has a long /iː/ sound.
These words have the same sound. Listen.
Put a line under the long sound.

cheese meat sweet eat meal week
beans clean teeth

▭ Listen again. Now you say the words.

Say these sentences:

I like meat and cheese in my evening meal.
I like to eat sweets.
I like to clean my teeth.

▭ Listen to the sentences on the cassette.

3 Sing a song! I love chocolate

▭ Look at page 91 in your Student's Book for the words to 'I love chocolate'.

Language focus

---

1 Say it clearly!

 All these words have the same sound. Listen and say the words.

/e/

any many pen when ten
get let west leg egg

Say these sentences.

Have you got any eggs?
Can you get ten pens?
An insect has six legs.

---

2 Talk to Linda

Talking about likes and dislikes

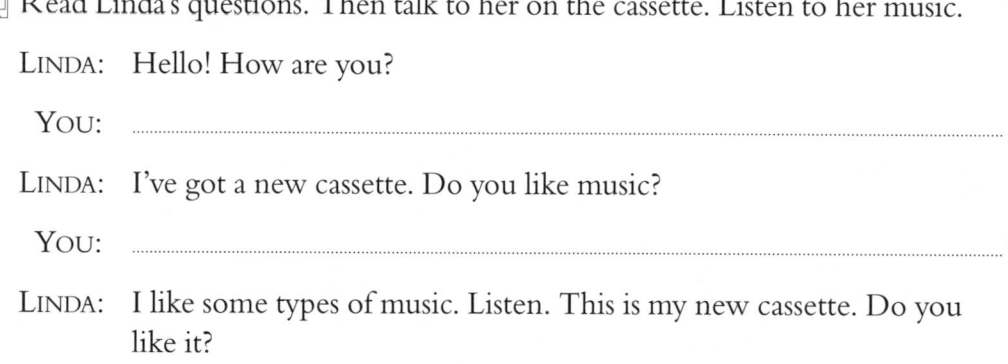 Read Linda's questions. Then talk to her on the cassette. Listen to her music.

LINDA: Hello! How are you?

YOU: ....

LINDA: I've got a new cassette. Do you like music?

YOU: ....

LINDA: I like some types of music. Listen. This is my new cassette. Do you like it?

YOU: ....

LINDA Oh no! It's the wrong cassette! This is my cassette. Do you like it?

YOU: ....

LINDA: I think it's really nice. Listen. This is my brother's music. What do you think?

YOU: ....

LINDA: Well, I don't mind it. Sometimes it's nice. He plays a lot of classical music. What's your favourite music?

YOU: ....

LINDA: Oh, yes. I like that too. I must go now. It's time to eat. Bye!

YOU: ....

9 Topic Into space

---

1 It's competition time!

Planets and the moon

You are on television. Listen and answer the questions.

MAN: Welcome to Star Quiz! I have six questions for you.
Number 1. How many planets are there?

YOU: ....

MAN: OK. And my next question is: can anything live on the moon?

YOU: ....

MAN: Excellent. Question 3. Why not?

YOU: ....

MAN: Yes. Because there isn't any air. Question 4. Why is the moon important
for ships?

YOU: ....

MAN: That's a difficult question! The moon makes the tides in the sea.
Two more questions. What is happening to the universe?

YOU: ....

MAN: That's difficult to understand. The universe is expanding. The stars are
moving. And now my last question. Question 6. Who were the first
people on the moon?

YOU: ....

MAN: Wonderful! Congratulations! Your prize is a trip to Planet Nevus for
two people!

---

2 Say it clearly!

/eɪ/

Listen. Say the words and the sentences. Open your mouth!

take   make   date   late   plate   hate   pancake   Light takes a long time to come from the stars.
The moon makes tides.   I hate pancakes!

---

3 Sing a song! Space

See page 91 in the Student's Book for the words.

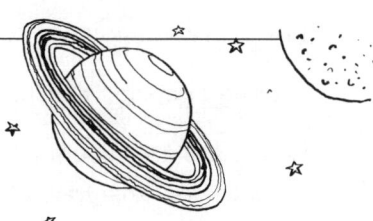

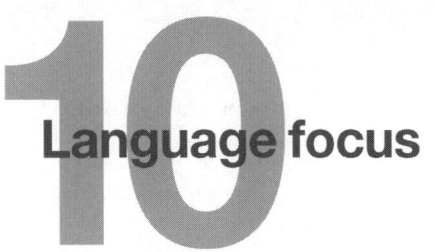

Language focus

---

1   In the bus station

Asking for travel information

You want to take a bus to Minton Town Centre tomorrow afternoon. You want to know:

- – the number of the bus
- – what time the bus goes
- – what time the bus comes back
- – how much the ticket costs

🔲 You go to the bus station. Listen and talk to the man.

MAN: Yes, can I help you?

YOU: *Can you tell* ....   ⟨bus?⟩

MAN: Yes. You can take bus 142.

YOU: ....

MAN: In the morning or in the afternoon?

YOU: ....   ⟨time?⟩

MAN: In the afternoon. Let me see. You can go at half past one
       or half past three.

YOU: ....   ⟨time back?⟩

MAN: There is a bus back at ten past two and ten past four.

YOU: ....   ⟨how much?⟩

MAN: How old are you?

YOU: ....

MAN: If you are under 15 it's £1.60.

YOU: ....   ⟨Thanks.⟩

MAN: You're welcome. Bye.

YOU: ....

---

2   Say it clearly!   /ɪŋ/

🔲 Listen. Say these words and sentences with '–ing'.

opening   getting   coming   putting   starting   waiting

He's opening the door.   He's coming down the ladder.   He's putting his foot on the moon.
I'm going to Planet Nevus tomorrow!

Topic 11 The cavepeople

1 A true story

Listening and drawing

Listen. The boys are telling a newspaper reporter about their adventure.

Draw the animals on the map.

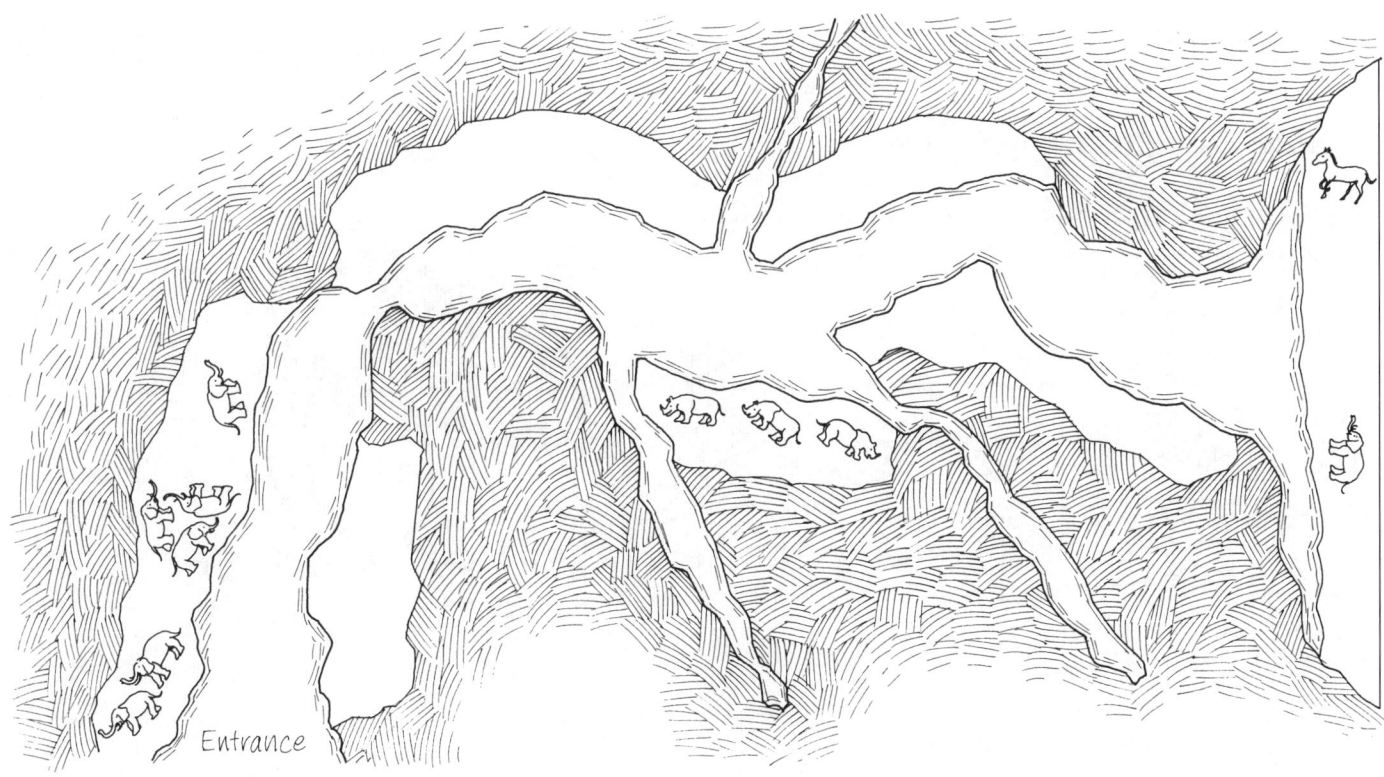

2 Talk to Linda

Write your answers to Linda's questions.

LINDA: What did you learn about in English this month?

YOU: ....

LINDA: Cavepeople! That's interesting! Did they have music like us?

YOU: ....

....

LINDA: That was clever! Did they have fire?

YOU: ....

....

LINDA: What did they eat and drink then?

YOU: ....

....

LINDA: Did the cavepeople live at the same time as dinosaurs?

YOU: ....

....

LINDA: You know a lot about cavepeople! I'm doing my maths homework now. Bye!

YOU: ....

Now talk to Linda on the cassette.

3 Sing a song! Caveman rock

See page 91 in the Student's Book for the words to 'Caveman rock'.

12 Language focus

---

1 Say it clearly!

/t/, /d/ and /ɪd/

There are three ways of saying '-ed' in English:

a 't' sound (/t/), example: washed   a 'd' sound (/d/), example: lived   an 'id' sound (/ɪd/), example: started

Listen. Say the verbs.

helped liked wanted decided asked stayed
visited changed studied looked watched played

washed /t/	lived /d/	started /ɪd/

Put the verbs in the columns. Check your answers with the cassette.

---

2 Talk to Linda

Talking about past events

Write some questions for Linda and some answers for her questions.

LINDA: Hi. Did you have a good weekend? I did. I went to the circus!

> where?

YOU: ....

LINDA: It was in my town. It was here for two days. I saw the clowns.

> funny?

YOU: ....

LINDA: Yes, they were. Then there were also some fire-eaters.

> frightening?

YOU: ....

LINDA: Yes! Then we went home and had a barbecue. Tell me about a fun weekend.

YOU: ....

LINDA: Oh! Were you with your friends?

YOU: ....

LINDA: Was there music?

YOU: ....

LINDA: Was there any nice food?

YOU: ....

LINDA: That sounds fun. I've got lots of homework now. Talk to you soon. Bye.

YOU: ....

Now talk to Linda on the cassette.

Extension

For more work on Unit 12, see Extension Exercise 5 on page 22.

Help yourself with pronunciation
Special Unit

1 Listen, look and repeat

Using a mirror

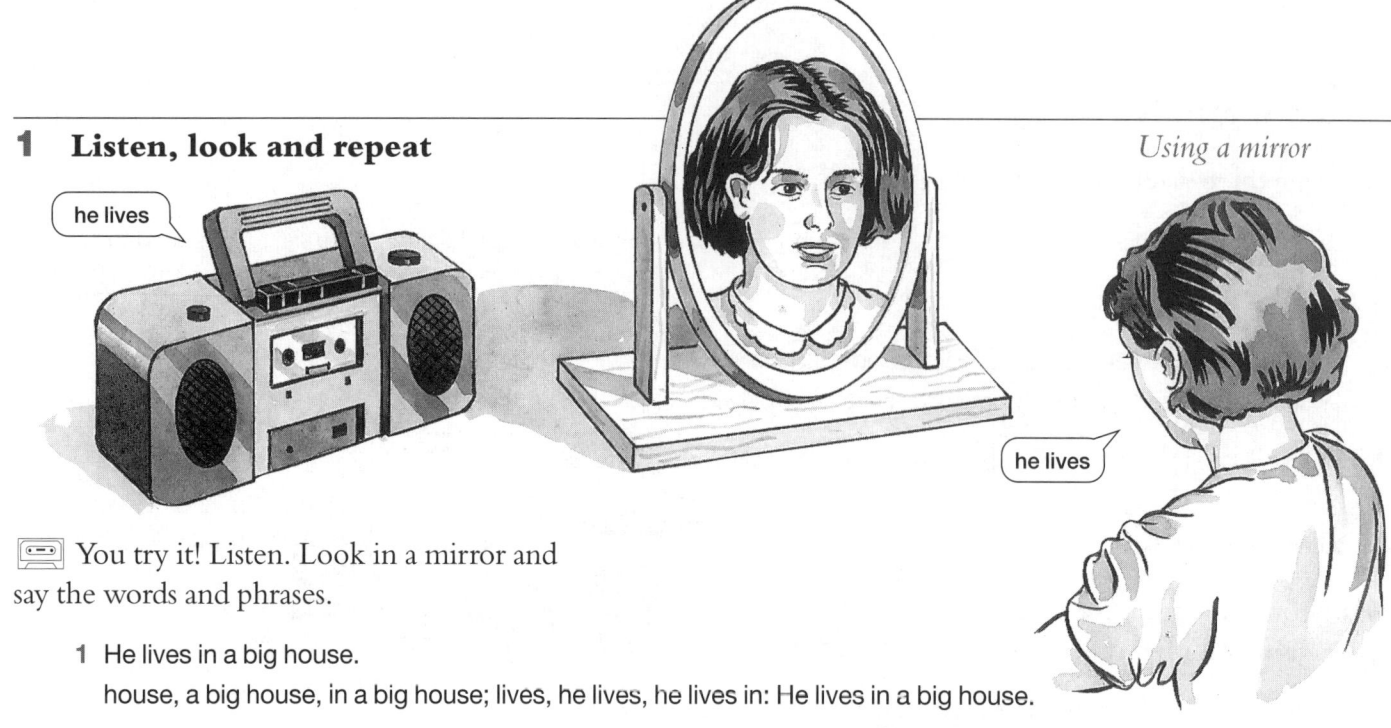

he lives

he lives

▱ You try it! Listen. Look in a mirror and
say the words and phrases.

1 He lives in a big house.

  house, a big house, in a big house; lives, he lives, he lives in: He lives in a big house.

2 Harry comes to school by bus.

  bus, by bus; to school, to school by bus; comes, Harry comes: Harry comes to school by bus.

2 Bang on the table!

Stress in two-syllable words

2.1 Words with two syllables

Here are some words with two syllables.
The first syllable is the strongest.
Say the words and bang your hand on
the table when you say the first syllable.

London
writing   jumping
hottest   longer
kitchen   teacher

London

<u>Lon</u>don   <u>wri</u>ting   <u>jum</u>ping   <u>hot</u>test   <u>lon</u>ger   <u>kit</u>chen   <u>tea</u>cher

2.2 Say the words

▱ Listen and say the words. Don't forget to bang the desk on the first syllable!

2.3 Some more words with two syllables

Look in the *Wordlist/Index* in your Student's Book.
Find some more two syllable words. Say them and
bang your hand on the first syllable.

parrot **sea**son **summ**er **au**tumn

---

3   What are the important words?

Stress in a sentence

3.1 Important words

In English, we say the important words strongest. Like this:

SOPHIE: Oh NO. When ARE you FREE?

MONA: Well, FRIDAY is FINE.

SOPHIE: OK. We can have the party THEN. Can you tell ALI?

📼 Listen. Say the dialogue.

3.2 Find a dialogue

Find a dialogue in your Student's Book.
Put a circle around the important words.

> MONA: Can you (tell) us which (bus) goes to (Bletchley) (Sportsground)?
> MAN: (Bletchley) (Sportsground). Well, you can (take) number (34).
> ALI: The (circus) (starts) at (half) past (three). What (time) is the (bus)?
> MAN: You can (take) one at (half) past (one) or (half) past (two).
> MONA: What (time) does the (bus) come (back)? (After) six (o'clock)?
> MAN: You can (take) one at (half) past (six) or (seven) (o'clock).
> SOPHIE: How (much) is the (ticket)?
> MAN: (Single) or (return)?
> SOPHIE: (Return).

3.3 Say the dialogue

Say the dialogue. Say the words in the circles stronger.

Listen to the dialogue on the cassette.
Do they say the words in the same way?

Well done!
Use the three ways to practise your pronunciation.

Extension exercises

1 Unit 3
Alice's letter

Listen. Alice is reading her letter. Are these sentences true (T) or false (F)?

1 ☐ Alice's school has 4000 students.
2 ☐ Alice has lunch at school.
3 ☐ Alice has lessons in the Science lab.
4 ☐ Alice has lessons in the Computer Room.
5 ☐ Alice plays football.
6 ☐ Alice plays basketball.

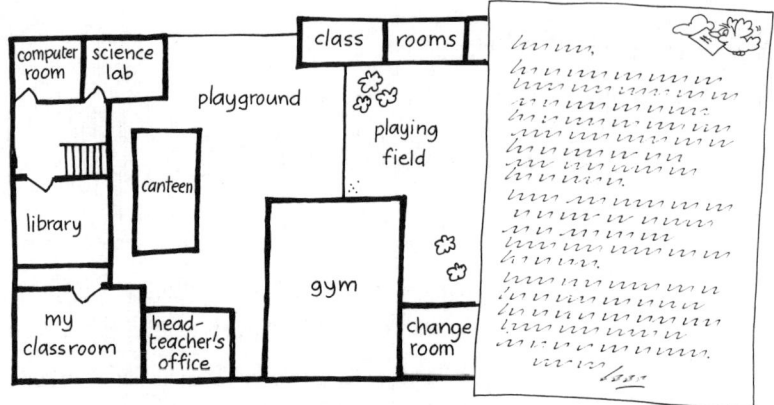

2 Unit 4
Talk to Linda

Write your answers to Linda's questions.

LINDA: Hi. My favourite schoolday is Monday. What's your favourite schoolday?

YOU: ....

LINDA: Why?

YOU: ....

LINDA: Oh. My favourite subject is Maths. Do you like Maths?

YOU: ....

LINDA: I have Maths every day. When do you have Maths?

YOU: ....

LINDA: What's your favourite weekend day?

YOU: ....

LINDA: Why?

YOU: ....

LINDA: Really? I like weekends. I can listen to music all day!

Talk to Linda on the cassette.

3　Unit 6
Humming birds

🔊 Listen. Can you complete the text?

Humming birds are very beautiful animals. They live in

.... and ....

.... They move their .... very fast. they

can stay in the same place .... for a

long time. They drink from .... They also eat

....

4　Unit 6
Come to my party!

🔊 There is a new student at your school. Write your answers and then talk
to him. Invite him to your birthday party!

PETER:　Hello. My name's Peter.

YOU:　..

PETER:　Do you want a sweet?

YOU:　..

PETER:　I've got two more friends with your name. They live near the town centre.
Where do you live?

YOU:　..

PETER:　Oh. I don't know that area. Where is it near?

YOU:　..

PETER:　Oh yes.

YOU:　(*invite him to your birthday party*)

....

PETER:　Yes please! At what time?

YOU:　..

PETER:　Great. What's your telephone number?

YOU:　..

PETER:　My number is 232675. See you at the party! Bye.

YOU:　..

Colin's story

Last Saturday, Colin had an adventure in a cave.
He is telling a newspaper reporter about it. Listen and
complete the reporter's notes.

Day: ....

His friends were ....

The weather was ....

The first cave was ....

He saw a river and he decided

to ....

In the second cave ....

....

He was in the cave for about ....

You can look at page 31 in your Workbook to check your answers.

Acknowledgements

The authors and publishers are grateful to the following illustrators and photographic sources:

Illustrators: Sophie Allington: pp. 9, 12*t*, 21*b*; Robert Calow: pp. 5*t*, 7*b*; Richard Deverell: p. 15*b*; Gecko Limited: all DTP illustrations and graphics; Steve Lach: pp. 18, 19; Colin Mier: pp. 10*t*, 17; John Plumb: p. 20*b*; Debbie Ryder: pp. 5*b*, 11*b*, 13*b*, 16*b*; Chris Ryley: pp. 4, 6, 7*t*, 8, 10*m*, 11*t*, 12*b*, 15*t*, 21*t*, 22*t*; John Storey: p. 13*t*.

Photographic sources: Nigel Luckhurst: pp. 14, 20*t*.

t = top   *m* = middle   *b* = bottom   *r* = right
c = centre   *l* = left

Picture research by Sandie Huskinson-Rolfe of PHOTOSEEKERS.